Guidelines
for Living

Guidelines for Living

HAROLD J. SALA

BAKER BOOK HOUSE
Grand Rapids, Michigan 49506

Copyright 1982 by
Baker Book House Company

ISBN: 0-8010-8219-6

Printed in the United States of America

Unless otherwise specified, Scripture references are from the
New International Version of the Bible, copyright 1978 by New
York International Bible Society.

Contents

Part Three

Great Lives Demonstrate Christianity Works

Part Four

The Principles of Success

Preface

Comedian Woody Allen is an atheist, and no matter how much he makes people laugh, when it comes to thoughts of dying, Allen doesn't have much to say that is humorous. He's afraid of death, and he doesn't mind saying so. He feels that death brings the end—total annihilation! Trying to comfort him, a friend said, "But aren't you happy that you will achieve immortality through your achievements?"

"Who cares about achieving immortality through achievements?" replied Allen. "I'm interested in achieving immortality through not dying."

Only one man had that prerogative—Jesus Christ. His power over death made Him the world's most influential person. His biography is cradled in the world's most influential book, the Bible, and together these two great forces have changed the course of all history touching the lives of all kinds of men. That's what this book is about!

All that we know about Christ, apart from a few scattered references in the writings of secular historians, comes from the pages of the Bible, and it is here that Christianity stands or falls. Yet when it comes to reasons for our faith, reasons as to why we accept the Bible as the inspired and infallible Word of God, most Christians are strangely silent. "Believe it because I said so!" parents tell their children. Lacking a foundation for their faith, these youth often "sell out" intellectually when their faith is assaulted by the claims of a secular society.

For nearly twenty years I have been producing two radio programs which are translated into fourteen languages and are released some nine hundred times weekly in English in more than forty countries. The correspondence which has come to my desk from every major area of the world tells me that men of every race and culture want answers to the questions of the heart. The selections in this book were written to confront the questions, and I trust that these selections will answer your questions, too.

Settle it in your mind once and for all—the Bible provides guidelines for living.

Part One

The Book with a Formula for Success

1
The Influence of the Bible

An eminent sociologist recently made the statement that the Bible is the most powerful weapon for the renewal of society that the world has ever seen. That's quite a statement in light of the fact that in the past thirty years we have had the greatest explosion of education and technical know-how in man's history. Today we have jet-age travel, allowing a person to cross a continent in a few hours; we have space exploration, taking man into the unknown; we have government and national welfare programs; education grants; foreign-aid programs—but down where we live in the hard, bitter world of reality, are these things really changing lives for the better?

The sociologist that I just quoted says, "Not enough." To back up his position, he offers a host of statistics that indicate crime, hatred, violence, and turmoil are increasing on a worldwide scale. The best-educated man in the world, whose life is wretchedly unhappy, hasn't really succeeded! This sociologist also believes that the Bible shows the only way that man can achieve a vertical relationship.

Let me illustrate the point. For a moment this sociologist wouldn't suggest that we abandon the struggle for education. He's not in favor of eliminating aid to undeveloped countries and needy people. He believes that if a man is hungry, you ought to give him something to eat. But he considers these to be horizontal relationships. It isn't enough to meet the physical needs of a man because man is more than an animal.

This accounts for the fact that so many people who are wealthy and have no material needs whatsoever are far from happy. J. Paul Getty, once the richest man in all the world, often said that he was unhappy and would be willing to trade his wealth for real happiness. You need more than simply having enough food, a shirt on your back, and shelter over your head. You need a vertical relationship that plants your feet firmly on the ground and helps you look beyond yourself to God. The Bible does this. It tells us that there is more to life than the "what's in it for me" attitude you may be living with. It tells us that beyond our human understanding God so loves us that He gave His only Son that we might live eternally. This fact, says a leading sociologist, can change a man's life. Time and time again, it has been visibly demonstrated.

Several years ago a colporteur (a man who distributes Bibles and Christian literature) went into a town in Brazil and sold a Bible to a man. A city official in the little town suspected the colporteur of distributing propaganda, so the official seized the Bible and threw it in the street. A local merchant picked it up and tore out the pages to wrap his customers' small purchases of onions, beans, rice, and other food items. Hungry for anything to read, the people read every word on their "grocery sacks" and then exchanged pages with friends and neighbors. Some gave their hearts to God and began telling others about God's love in sending His Son. Months later when a missionary reached the town, he found a living church and a house full of new converts.

The Bible is the most powerful means of changing hearts in a hard world. It is God's prescription for right living. It contains the guidelines we so desperately need to live as God intended we should live.

The man who is ignorant of the Bible is ignorant of the most significant fact in world history—Christ's coming; the most influential people in history—Israel; the most influential Person in history—Jesus Christ; and the basis of a well-adjusted, successful life. It is an ignorance you can't afford to have.

2

The Uniqueness
of Scripture

"How do I know that the Bible is different from any other book?" This is a good question. It was asked by a high-school student who had just become interested in the world's most widely-printed book. There are lots of intelligent men and women today who may not be quite brave enough to voice a question that may exist in their hearts. It isn't necessarily that these people are atheists—in fact, they very much believe in the existence of God. Like the high-school student, in sincerity, they want to know how the Bible is different from any other book. Over the years I have answered the question by giving six reasons why I accept Scripture as a book that is unique.

The first unique characteristic is that the Bible is scientifically accurate in the statements that it makes. To me, this is nothing short of divine providence. Remember, though, that the Bible isn't a textbook on science; it is a textbook on living. Yet the statements of Scripture can be harmonized with the findings of modern science. Let me give you an example. Psalm 103:12 says that when God forgives a person, his sins are removed as far as the east is from the west. This is significant in that if David had said the north and the south, it would have been a distance of some 12,420 miles, but when God says the east and the west, it is good news, for the east and west never meet.

The second reason that I accept the Bible as unique is because of the fulfilled prophecy that it contains. Can you discount the predictive element of the Bible? I don't think so. Time and time again the prophets predicted certain events would take place, and hundreds of years later those events transpired with such complete accuracy that it would seem the prophet actually had been describing the event as a witness. I will list a few examples. A thousand years before the time of Christ, David told that Christ would be crucified, and that He would cry, "My God, my God, why hast thou forsaken me?" (KJV).

David's prophecy, found in Psalm 22, was fulfilled to the letter. Seven centuries before Christ was ever born, Isaiah told that the Savior would be born of a virgin. In Isaiah 53, the prophet vividly foretold His suffering, and these things were graphically fulfilled. The prophet Micah even pinpointed the city of Bethlehem as the place of Christ's birth— that was how the wise men knew where to come. Things such as this couldn't have just happened.

The third reason that I give for accepting Scripture as the Word of God is its indestructibility. No other book has been so carefully preserved and passed from generation to generation. There have been many attempts to destroy it. In the year A.D. 303 the Roman emperor Diocletian ordered every Bible to be burned, and the streets of ancient Rome were lighted by bonfires as Bibles were burned. In recent years Communist dictators have attempted to thwart sales of the Bible, yet one hundred thousand people recently lined up in the streets of Moscow when the government approved the sale of a Bible story book.

The fourth reason that I give for accepting the authority of the Bible is the unity of Scripture. For a moment, keep in mind that the

Bible was written by some forty men over a period of sixteen hundred years, yet there is one theme and one purpose. In each and every book I see God meeting the needs of men and showing them how to live.

The fifth reason I give for accepting the validity of Scripture is manuscript evidence, which I shall discuss at length in the next two chapters.

The last reason why I accept the Bible as infallible is because of personal experience. I've found that God keeps His word and comes through with what He promises. Time and time again, I have appropriated His promises and found that God will do what He has promised in His Word. Christ said, "Him that cometh to me I will in no wise cast out" (John 6:37, KJV). I came and He received me; He'll do the same thing for you, as you read His Word and apply it to your heart. Don't take anyone else's word for what the Bible says—read it and discover guidelines for living.

3

The Great
Treasure Hunt, 1

When Sir Walter Scott, the great British poet, lay dying, he made an urgent request. "Bring me the Book. Bring me the Book." But since he owned a vast library, those who were around his bed were not quite sure which book he was requesting. Anxious to comply with his last wishes, they leaned over and asked, "Which book do you mean?" Impatiently he said, "There is only one book, the Bible. Bring me the Book."

Revered by some and railed upon by others, "the Book," as Scott called it, has endured the test of time. Why? Why this book when others have but taken their place in libraries and been lost in oblivion? To say that it is a living book, inspired by God, is almost trite to the skeptic, yet almost every year produces additional scientific evidence documenting the validity of the text. One of the most convincing arguments for the validity of the Book is the continuing plethora of documentary textual evidence—manuscripts and ancient documents containing the writings of Scripture which can be compared and collated with the text of our modern Bible.

How do you know that men haven't tampered with the Bible and changed it so that it is no longer what the apostles wrote? For example, perhaps well-meaning individuals (or some not-so-well-meaning) didn't like what they found and decided to improve upon the text. Logic says that if you went back to an earlier manuscript or copy of Scripture, the earlier document would prove that someone changed the text. That, simply put, is how the science of higher criticism developed.

The search for the earliest manuscripts is a fascinating treasure hunt to the person who is interested in the Bible. The great treasure hunt often spans centuries, with individuals making their contribution before passing across the stage of life. Take, for instance, the search for Codex Sinaiticus, one of the four finest manuscripts of the Bible, written in Greek about A.D. 400. Originally the manuscript (which you understand was a handwritten copy of the Bible) was penned by a scribe for one of the churches; however, it was eventually taken to St. Catherine's Monastery in Sinai, where it was deposited for safekeeping. Its keeping was so safe that the monks there entirely forgot about it, and the centuries began to roll by. The valuable manuscript was lost in the shuffle of thousands of scrolls kept in the library until 1844, when Constantine von Tischendorf visited St. Catherine's Monastery in search of ancient copies of the Bible.

While Tischendorf was in the library, he noticed 129 leaves of a very old manuscript lying in a paper basket. The old pieces of parchment had been put there for the monks to use to light the fire on chilly mornings. The writing immediately caught the scholar's attention. He looked intently. Yes, it was old, very old. Tischendorf's excitement began to rise. The more he studied the pieces of old manuscript, the more excited he was. He had found leaves which were part of a Bible, or a manuscript, written about A.D. 400. Tischendorf was given 43 of these leaves, but his time had run out, and he had to leave the monastery.

But the treasure hunt continued fifteen years later, when Tischendorf returned to the site of his first discovery. To his horror, the 86 leaves or pages which Tischendorf had to leave behind in 1844 couldn't be found. The monks, not sensing their importance, had mislaid them. No matter how they searched, the leaves could not be found. The night before Tischendorf was to leave, the man who had been his host showed him a codex, thinking this might be the missing document. It was! He found not only the 86 leaves left behind fifteen years before, but also another 112 leaves of the Old Testament, the entire New Testament, and two other documents from the ancient church.

4
The Great
Treasure Hunt, 2

The search for the early manuscripts of the Bible is like a great treasure hunt that spans the centuries. Constantine von Tischendorf was the principal character in an exciting drama that produced one of the four finest Greek manuscripts of the Bible.

In 1844 the scholar discovered a portion of a very old manuscript which had been placed in a basket by the fire at St. Catherine's Monastery in Sinai. To his horror, the leaves of this very old manuscript of the Bible were to be used in lighting the blaze. Fifteen years later Tischendorf was able to return. When one of the monks invited Tischendorf to his cell for a cup of tea, defeat was turned to victory. As the monk took some leaves of a manuscript from a bag in which they had been stored, Tischendorf recognized these as being some of the leaves he had seen before.

Tischendorf was thrilled beyond words. This time he wanted to insure that the manuscripts weren't lost as the initial discovery was after his 1844 visit. He bought the documents, or codex, for the equivalent of about seven thousand dollars, and took it to Russia. It was presented to Czar Alexander II, who had financed Tischendorf's expedition. The manuscript remained at the Imperial Library of St. Petersburg until 1933 when the Communist government, not being interested in Bibles, sold the document to the British Museum for one hundred thousand pounds sterling or about a half million dollars. But that isn't the end of the treasure hunt.

This time the scene is the same—St. Catherine's Monastery deep in the Sinai, now under Israel's control. The Greek Orthodox monks who have been there for centuries are still there, and so are some missing leaves from the book, or codex, which is now identified as Codex Sinaiticus, the same one first identified by Tischendorf. The most recent find in the continuing drama was made in 1976, but has just come to the attention of the public.

A few years ago the monks decided to make some renovations to the monastery, which has been undisturbed since its founding in the second or third century, and began tearing out a wall. To their surprise and delight they found a storage cavity containing thousands of fragments or pieces of manuscripts—enough to fill forty-seven large cartons. Among these manuscripts were at least eight additional leaves or pages from the manuscript which Tischendorf originally found; at least four of the eight are from the Old Testament Book of Genesis.

Undoubtedly Constantine von Tischendorf would have been delighted. Millions of sincere men and women around the world applaud the dedicated efforts of scholars who study these ancient texts. "Why bother with something so old?" someone might ask, and the answer is simple. If our contemporary Bibles are substantially the same as those written in the first few centuries of the Christian church, we can be relatively sure that the Bible, as we know it, was in the main passed down through the centuries without change.

When contemporary scholars compare the ancient texts with our modern versions, they are quick to admit that there are no major changes in our Bible from the Bibles of the second century. I am convinced that God has allowed the unearthing of some of these very old manuscripts, including the discoveries at Qumran, to encourage men and women to trust the Book and to disallow the claims of some today who would have you believe the Bible isn't a reliable book.

The miracle of preservation is often overlooked, but, believe me, you'll find God's presence and guiding hand right there preserving the documents that were slated to be used to light fires on a cold Sinai morning. As Sir Walter Scott put it, "There is only one book, the Bible."

5
The Story
Manuscripts Tell

Today Bible scholars have at their finger-
tips literally thousands of manuscripts and
related documents upon which the study of
the Word is based. The Greek scholar A. T.
Robertson said there are eight thousand
manuscripts of the Latin Vulgate Bible, and at
least one thousand of other versions. The
latest count, according to Bruce Metzger, is
that we have about five thousand Greek
manuscripts of the Bible, and we have more
than thirteen thousand ancient portions of the
New Testament. Compare that pile of manuscripts with ten copies of Caesar's *Gallic War*,
which was written about the same time as the
New Testament was. Of the ancient Greek
classics, there are fewer than a dozen good
manuscripts, which are considered to be of
great value.

What kind of a story does a single manuscript of the Bible tell? The story is a fascinating one, and although you may not fully understand what a scholar would, you can still appreciate the individual contribution that each, and all of them, have to make to the validity of our Bibles. First, the kind of writing on each manuscript is like the black box that has the history of an airplane's flight. It tells something of the locality or the place where the manuscript was written, in that the penmanship found in the various places— Caesarea on the coast of Israel, or Alexandria in Egypt—differed.

The type of writing also gives some indication as to the time of the writing. In earlier days the manuscripts were written in a rough, flowing style or in large characters, according to Clarence Thiessen; in later manuscripts the style became polished and more exact as scribes took greater care in their writing.

The materials that the manuscripts were written on add something to the story as well. If a manuscript is written on papyrus (and it is generally believed that the original New Testament books were written on papyrus), it usually indicates that the manuscript was written from the first to the fourth century.

The words *vellum* and *parchment* are used almost interchangeably today, but there is a difference. Vellum, the skin of calves or antelope, was used from the fourth to the ninth century for writing materials, and parchment, the skin of sheep or goats, was used after the ninth century.

Studying these ancient manuscripts is a science, and as such it's known as textual criticism, a term that seems to imply more than it really is. Scholars want to produce as accurate a Bible as possible; good men aren't intent on destroying it. They want the same thing you do—the Word of God in its simplicity and purity. In analyzing the various manuscripts, these scholars have come up with some ground rules that, at first, seem to baffle the average person, but as you think about them, you will come to discern their wisdom.

The first rule is to accept the reading or the manuscript which best explains the origin of the others. The second is to accept the more difficult reading. Why? Because it's the tendency of human nature to change the text or add a few words explaining what is hard to understand. The third rule is to decide generally for the shorter reading, since scribes often tried to help the Holy Spirit by adding their comments. The fourth rule is to accept that reading that is most characteristic of the one who wrote the book, and the fifth is to discount readings that are manifestly peculiar to a scribe or copier.

"It should be emphasized," writes Thiessen, "that concerning the great bulk of the words in the New Testament there is complete agreement among textual critics." May I summarize the point? When you pick up your Bible, do it with confidence that the words stamped on its cover—*Holy Bible*—are an accurate description of the contents. Realize that God has given us thousands and thousands of manuscripts which support the fact that the Bible was given by the inspiration of God. It's God's authoritative Word. So put it to work in your life.

6
Archaeology and
Bible History, 1

Webster's dictionary defines archaeology as "the scientific study of ancient cultures and peoples." The word *archaeology* itself comes from two Greek words, *archaios*, meaning "ancient," and *logos* or *logia*, meaning "the study of." Hence, archaeology has developed into the scientific discipline which studies the material remains of past human life and activities. Archaeology goes back to the year 1799, when Napoleon led his army into the rich Nile River valley, and the Rosetta stone was found, which proved to be the key to understanding Egyptian hieroglyphics. But it has actually been in this century that the modern science has come into its own.

While some people think of archaeology as the process of taking a shovel and seeing what can be unearthed, nothing could be further from the truth. Anyone with a slight knowledge of what archaeology is all about is quick to recognize that it is work, painfully slow work, and has great rewards if you are interested in uncovering the remains of the past. An area to be excavated is carefully measured and photographed, and then under the scrutiny of scientists the ground is carefully measured into squares, forming a wafflelike pattern. When the soil is removed, it isn't removed with shovels. Often tools that are as small as a toothbrush are used. Then the refuse is sifted and even washed to produce every shred of evidence.

When something is found before it is removed from the ground, it is photographed and often cast in plaster of Paris to insure that it will not be lost to posterity. What does the archaeologist search for? Everything that lies buried beneath the surface of the ground, but principally pieces of pottery, which can be dated from their materials, design, and artistic pattern; coins; cooking utensils; weapons; clothes, which are extremely rare; grains or foods; pieces of parchment or tablets, such as were recently unearthed at Aleppo in Syria.

As archaeology has developed into a secular, scientific discipline, it has done more to confirm the historical statements of the Bible than perhaps any other branch of science does. Merrill F. Unger is a scholar and archaeologist whose books are widely read. Speaking of the role of archaeology in confirming biblical data, Unger says,

> . . . archaeology has an important role in authenticating the Bible both generally and specifically. Generally, scientific archaeology has exploded many extreme theories and false assumptions that used to be paraded in scholarly circles as settled facts. But no longer can higher criticism dismiss the Hebrew patriarchs as mere legendary figures or deny that Moses could write, or assert that Mosaic legislation is anachronistic for such an early age. These and other extreme options have been proved completely untenable by archaeological research.

Does archaeology prove the Bible? I have come to the conclusion that you cannot prove anything to anyone who refuses to accept evidence, but to the sincere, unbiased mind the evidence of archaeology is explicit confirmation of the accuracy of the historical data found in the Bible. To me archaeology is one of the truly significant contributions of science in confirming the record that you find in Scripture, but ultimately a man accepts the Bible as the Word of God by faith—not by proof. The ultimate demonstration of validity is a personal one as you discover what God says about your life and discover that it is 100 percent true.

7
Archaeology and
Bible History, 2

A team of Italian archaeologists working in Syria struck it rich. What they found wouldn't have brought much joy to the heart of a prospector, but when these archaeologists unearthed a room in part of an ancient palace and found that this room had been used to store ancient clay tablets, they were ecstatic with joy. One of them told the press, "When we saw the room and the mass of tablets we had the feeling as if the librarian had locked the door and left yesterday at five o'clock. . . . That's when we got hysterical."

Why should pieces of old clay tablets be so important in the world of supersonic jets? Those old clay tablets are important and worth an estimated $15 million because they are the most extensive recent find that sheds light on ancient Near Eastern civilization, and the information found on these fifteen thousand tablets will result in the rewriting of the history books dealing with this part of the world.

It all started when a team of archaeologists from the University of Rome began digging into a tell (Tell Mardikh) south of Aleppo. Incidentally, a tell is a mound of earth which holds remains of a bygone civilization. To an archaeologist a tell is an encyclopedia of information about people who lived a long time ago, and as one of the branches of modern science, archaeology has become a scientific investigation and analysis of the remains of ancient civilizations. For centuries men walked over these mounds, not realizing their tremendous significance, but in modern times men have learned that the spade of the archaeologist can unearth a nearly complete history of a people, show the way they lived, and reconstruct many of the accouterments of a civilization.

In 1975 the Italian archaeologists unearthed a royal palace which was in the ancient city of Ebla (near the modern city of Aleppo, Syria). Because the process of unearthing remains buried for thousands of years is very, very slow, the archaeologists were able to unearth only three walls of the room where the fifteen thousand documents were stored. Excavations resumed in 1976, but at the present time only a small section of the royal palace has been excavated. The archive room where the important finds were made may have been adjacent to the main library, but as of this date the main library has yet to be discovered. The tablets that were discovered were stacked vertically on wooden shelves. They vary from the size of the palm of a man's hand to that of a large brick. The tablets are important primarily because they tell of a large Syrian empire which rivaled ancient Egypt and Mesopotamia sometime about 2250 B.C. An entire empire had been lost to history until the spade of the archaeologist unearthed it. Most of the tablets, 80 percent in fact, are accounts of economic and commercial transactions—bills and invoices much the same as the ones we use today. The rest cover a vast number of subjects such as treaties, military reports, religious writings, descriptions of sacrifices and religious rites (including stories of creation and the great flood)—all of this taking place more than four thousand years ago.

How does the recent find relate to the

historical position of the Bible? If the Bible is historically accurate, then it should follow that the spade of the archaeologist should produce only evidence that confirms, not conflicts, with the record of Scripture. Of interest to me is that the findings of the modern archaeologists have largely confirmed the historical evidence of the Bible, often shedding much light on portions of Scripture that were scoffed at by secular historians.

8

The Biblical Significance of the Ebla Find

More than four thousand years ago—approximately 2230 B.C.—King Naram-Sin of Akkad, one of the great Mesopotamian states, led an army against a rival king whose great empire was at Ebla, near the modern city of Aleppo in Syria. The attacking king was from one of the city-states in Mesopotamia, where civilization may have had its genesis. When the fire from the battle subsided, the royal palace of Ebla was destroyed, and the soldiers looted and burned what remained. The king was killed or deposed and the city was destroyed. Some of the residents were taken back to Akkad in chains, and others scattered, trying to start their lives over again. Vultures circled over the ruins and the Syrian wind began to blow, piling dust and dirt over the remains. In a few years the ruins were hardly visible and eventually there was nothing evident—only a mound covered with sand. That was the way the center of a great civilization vanished until the spade of a team of Italian archaeologists from the University of Rome unearthed the palace and remains of Ebla in the 1970s. Many people wonder how a great city could so completely vanish from the world, yet history tells us that it has happened more than once.

In recent years the modern science of archaeology has begun to reconstruct life in these ancient cities so completely that the inhabitants would undoubtedly have been amazed. What is important about the Ebla find is that a great empire, which rivaled ancient Egypt and Mesopotamia, is rediscovered. This great empire stretched from what is now Turkey on the south to Iraq on the east. The fifteen thousand tablets found in Tell Mardikh shed a great deal of light on the way the people lived and the way the government was operated. One tablet recorded an international treaty, the oldest known in history, between Ebla and the city of Assur, providing for the establishment of a free trade area. The treaty included a variety of commercial and legal provisions, including some for crimes.

Of significance to the student of Scripture is the fact that one tablet contained a vocabulary of Sumerian words, including an explanation of how Sumerian words are pronounced. The Sumerians were a non-Semetic people who developed writing about 3000 B.C.; they played an important part in the development of biblical culture. Among names found there are biblical names such as Abraham, Ishmael, and David. Says Professor Giovanni Pettinato, a linguist who has been reading the tablets, "The Ebla tablets establish the patriarchs and their names as historical realities. And they seem to show that many Hebrew ideas and words came from Ebla. We wondered," says the professor, "why the Bible calls judges and rulers before the kings. Now we know that in Ebla the leaders of the conquered cities were called judges."

Pettinato believes that biblical Hebrew may be traced to the language of ancient Ebla—a claim that will be widely disputed by other linguists. Nonetheless, the tablets contain the names of biblical sites such as Hazor, Megiddo, Gaza, and even Jerusalem *(Urusalima)* as exporting sites.

Chalk up another important find as the spade of the archaeologist confirms the record of God's Word, the Bible.

Part Two

The One
Who Taught
the Way

9
What Did Jesus Look Like?

It's an amazing fact, yet true. The writers of the four Gospels never gave to the world a description of what Jesus Christ looked like, and there's a reason for this, which I'll share at the end of this chapter. Nonetheless, there is a document that supposedly contains an actual description of Christ. It says:

There lives at this time in Judea a man of singular virtue—whose name is Jesus Christ— whom the barbarians esteem as a prophet, but his followers love and adore him as the offspring of the immortal God. He calls back the dead from the graves and heals all sorts of diseases with a word or touch.

He is a tall man, well-shaped, and of an amiable and reverend aspect; he has hair of a

45

color that can hardly be matched, falling into graceful curls, waving about and very agreeably couching about his shoulders, parted on the crown of his head, running as a stream to the front after the fashion of the Nazarites; his forehead high, large, and imposing; his cheeks without spot or wrinkle, beautiful with a lovely red; his nose and mouth formed with exquisite symmetry; his beard of a color suitable to his hair, reaching below his chin and parted in the middle like a fork; his eyes bright blue, clear, and serene, look innocent, dignified, manly, and mature.

In proportion of body most perfect and captivating; his arms and hands delectable to behold. He rebukes with majesty, counsels with mildness; his whole address, whether in word or deed, being eloquent and grave. No man has seen him laugh, yet his manners are exceedingly pleasant, but he has wept frequently in the presence of men. He is temperate, modest, and wise, a man for his extraordinary beauty and divine perfection, surpassing the children of men in every sense.

There you have it—a description said to have been written by an eyewitness. But the question is, "Can we believe that it is authentic? Or is it a clever forgery?" Although scholars would like to accept it as genuine, this document is generally believed to have been brought to the Vatican sometime during the ninth century, when the practice of collecting religious relics was at its peak. Nonetheless, the spirit of what an unknown author wrote is consistent with the record of the four Gospels.

Each of the writers of the Gospels reflected a different point of view. The tax collector, Matthew, wrote from a Jewish point of reference, while Mark reflected a Roman viewpoint. Luke, the Gentile physician, who was probably from Syria, presented Christ as the perfect man, reflecting a Grecian viewpoint. John, whose Gospel describes events taking place in twenty-one days in the life of Jesus, spoke of Jesus as the Son of God—the Savior for all men of all ages.

When we compare what the four wrote, there is a great deal of information yet no description of what Jesus really looked like. Why? Apparently God wanted us to realize that what Jesus did is far more important than what He looked like, and for this reason no artist ever gave to posterity a painting of the face of Jesus; no sculptor ever left His features chiseled in stone or cast in bronze, but the world will never escape the fact that this one, born of a virgin in Bethlehem, was crucified at the hands of the Roman soldiers, placed in a tomb, and rose the third day. When it is all said and done, what Jesus did will forever be more important than what He looked like.

10
Profiles of the Face of Jesus

From impressions made on the walls of the catacombs of Rome to paintings in the mansions of the wealthy, Jesus Christ has been the inspiration of the world's greatest artists. Rubens, Raphael, da Vinci, Titian, Michelangelo, and thousands of others have all taken brush and palette in hand and painted the face of Jesus as they pictured it in their minds.

Copies of Warren Salman's painting of the face of Christ hang in many homes, yet when I finally cross heaven's threshold, for some reason I don't expect Christ to look just like the image portrayed by Salman. Visit Saint Paul's Cathedral in London and there you will find Holman Hunt's famous painting of Christ standing at the door and knocking. Climb into a jeepney in the Philippines, and chances are you will see a picture of the face of Jesus. But what does Christ really look like?

If you want to discover what Jesus looks like, you must turn to the pages of the Gospels and read what His biographers wrote —men who walked with Jesus for three years and experienced the impact of His life on theirs. Did they actually tell us what Jesus looked like? No, but they did give to all mankind profiles of the face of Jesus—profiles which allow us to see beneath the physiognomy and discover the real man.

The picture that you develop may be different from mine, but the person will be the same. As I read the Gospels and ask myself what Jesus looked like, the first profile that develops in my mind is a profile of compassion—Jesus reached out to men and women who were neglected and ignored by others, and felt what they felt. He suffered as they suffered. He touched the untouchables—the leper, the widow, the blind beggar—men and women with whom I can identify.

Another profile that becomes apparent is the profile of tenderness. Unlike weakness, tenderness reveals sensitivity. Jesus related to children, yet was a man who could take a whip and drive the moneychangers from the temple. His face undoubtedly revealed strength of character and firmness. Jesus had depth of personality that revealed real love for men and women.

Other profiles I see are those of purity, suffering, compelling love, justice, empathy, and a score of other virtues and emotions. When I see Jesus I don't expect someone to take me by the hand and lead me to Him, saying, "Sala, I want to introduce you to Jesus." You see, twenty-eight years ago someone introduced me to Him, and although I have never seen Him in the flesh, I know Him, for He has walked with me and guided my life. John said, "When he appears, we shall be like him, for we shall see him as he is" (I John 3:2).

Jesus Christ has become all things to all races and all people. He's Oriental to the Japanese, He's black to the Africans. He's an Easterner to the Russians. But to all, He is the Son of God who became flesh and lived among us. He's the glory of the Father, the second person of the Trinity, the One who ever lives to intercede for those who will believe in Him.

How do you picture Jesus? Maybe you've gotten your impression second- or third-hand. You've never taken time to develop your own profile of Him by turning the pages of Scripture, one at a time. Since Christ is alive, you can meet Him as have countless millions, and you can learn that to know Him is to love Him.

11
The Hands
of Christ

A friend of mine who is a mathematics professor tells how she met the board of trustees
of the college for an interview before she was
hired. As soon as she was seated the board
members asked her to remove her gloves and
place her hands on the table. Strange request?
Not really, for those men realized that your
hands reveal a great deal about your character
and life.

A doctor once told me that when he talks
with patients he notices their hands, for their
hands tell him almost as much as his stethoscope does, and hands share some secrets that
a stethoscope will never reveal.

Nervous hands tell of a fretful disposition
and a proneness to worry. Rough, strong
hands speak of labor and toil. Tender, gentle

hands speak of a mother's love and care. Gnarled, wrinkled hands indicate the mellowing of age. Delicate, sensitive hands may speak of artistic ability.

Have you thought much about the hands of Jesus? His were hands that reached out to the needs of humanity; hands that held little children and blessed them; hands that touched the lame, the blind, the sick; hands that took a little boy's lunch and fed a multitude of perhaps fifteen thousand people; hands that were one day held to a Roman cross while nails were driven into them.

When Jesus healed someone, He often did something that seems strange to us today. He would reach out and would touch that person with His hand. He could have simply spoken the word; He could have commanded the sickness to depart, but He touched people. There was nothing magical about the hands of Christ. Is there a reason then for Christ's touching someone? I believe there is, for when Christ touched someone (unlike when you or I touch someone), God touched man.

By touching suffering humanity, Christ established a point of contact between man and God. The touch of the Master's hands brought healing to the emotions and minds of people. Actually people were no different two thousand years ago than they are today. They worried; they were fearful. Their lives were knotted by frustration and turmoil. They knew something of pressures, stress, and uneasiness, but when Christ touched a person, He brought peace to a distressed life.

Perhaps you are thinking, "Christ may have healed people two thousand years ago, but that's all over." Dr. Ralph Byron, chief of cancer surgery for one of the leading hospitals that specializes in cancer research and treatment, is a Christian. He says,

> I am certain that if the skeptics in the day of Christ would have brought blind, deaf, lepers, and paralytics to Him simply for a controlled experiment, He would not have healed them. Miracles are not performed to convince skeptics but to bring glory to God through the lives of those whom He so chooses to heal. For this purpose God works in miraculous ways today.

The touch of the Master still brings healing mentally and physically, but most important of all, it brings healing spiritually. Jesus healed men, but eventually they died. He raised men from the dead, but sooner or later they died.

When Christ healed a man spiritually, He gave to him the assurance that he would live forever. Christ is still in the business of touching lives.

12
Jesus Was
a Jew

When a Japanese Christian came to San Francisco for a visit, he attended a church service where Ralph Sockman spoke about the life of Jesus. Asked by a friend how he enjoyed the message, the guest replied, "Well, to hear him tell it, Jesus was an American, a Methodist, and an Armenian. But everyone knows that it is not true, for Jesus was really a Japanese, a Baptist, and a Calvinist."

While all men see Christ as a reflection of their own race and culture, Jesus was a Jew who could trace His lineage through His mother to King David. In recent times Jews around the world have been taking a new look at Jesus. For a long time, Jewish rabbis have looked at the life of Christ with contempt because they have associated Jesus with

Christians who have persecuted Jews; therefore, Jesus to them was an apostate and a false Messiah.

Newsweek magazine, commenting on what is happening, said, "Jewish scholars in the last fifteen years have quietly begun to recognize Jesus as a brother who spoke in faith to other Jews." The Israeli scholar Pinchas Lapide of Bar-Ilan University near Tel Aviv is quoted as saying that "Jesus was more loyal to the Torah than I am as an Orthodox Jew." Since 1948, Lapide has published more than 187 books, articles, essays, and poems about Jesus in relationship to Judaism. Although these Jewish scholars deny the virgin birth or the resurrection of Christ, associating these truths with Christian teaching, they see Jesus as a first-century rabbi and recognize the New Testament as a document which can tell them a great deal about Judaism of the first century. Nonetheless, in the past decade a great number of Jews have come to recognize Jesus as the Messiah and contend that they are more Jewish than ever before.

David Flusser, professor of religious history at Hebrew University, recently said, "I do not think that many Jews would object if the Messiah—when He came—was the Jew Jesus."

Flusser's candid statement is remarkable in itself. But the Jesus that most Jews consider is a caricature, not the Jesus portrayed in the pages of the New Testament. It has been my experience that most Jewish friends have never gone to the pages of the New Testament to discover what the Jewish authors of the Book had to say.

With the exception of Luke, who was probably a Gentile physician, every word in the New Testament was written by a first-century Jew; therefore, the New Testament is basically a Jewish document that contends the Man born in Bethlehem fulfills Old Testament prophecies concerning a Messiah. It is not by chance that many events taking place in the life of Christ were clearly foretold centuries before—such as the birth of Christ in Bethlehem, prophesied by Micah five hundred years before Christ, or the suffering and death of Christ predicted by Isaiah seven hundred years before Christ and by David in Psalm 22.

Is the expected coming of a Jewish Messiah one and the same as the second coming of Christ to the Christian? Christians believe it will be the same, and says Flusser, His coming may be welcomed by the Jewish community. If it is, then what Jewish disciples wrote about

Jesus is authentic and credible. "He came to that which was his own," wrote John, "but his own did not receive him. Yet to all who received him, to those who believed in his name, he gave the right to become children of God" (John 1:11-12). And it is this that really counts.

13
A Model
for Marxism

A surprising idea has sprouted in Communist Eastern Europe—that the character of Christ is the selfless model for Marxism. "Jesus Christ is not the enemy of this society," writes Romanian Baptist pastor, Josif Ton, "rather He is its only chance." Ton's thesis is that if people are only an evolutionary happenstance—a chance combination of matter —and their attitudes are shaped by the environment, there is no motive for morality. Rather he believes that greed and selfishness result.

"If Marxism is to work," reasons Ton, "then there must be a motive for character, for morality, a reason for high aspiration, a motive to give yourself for the welfare of other people." Jesus Christ, believes Ton, is the only answer and the only motive high enough to provide that kind of behavior. He says, "In Scripture and in history, we can see that wherever the spirit of Christ's teaching was accepted and assimilated in its totality, the result was a noble life put to the service of the common good, even at the cost of self-sacrifice."

And how has Ton's thesis been received by the Romanian government? His books have been seized, and he has undergone extensive interrogation by government authorities. After repeated beatings by the Romanian authorities, Ton prepared to make the supreme sacrifice—that of his life. "When you put your life on the altar, when you make ready and accept to die," he wrote, "you are invincible." Following the publication of another paper saying that the noble goals of Marxism would never be attained apart from a deep commitment to God, authorities expelled Ton from his native land.

Traditionally, Marxism has espoused Jesus as a revolutionary hero, but never has embraced the teaching of Christ that demands commitment to a higher authority and power —God Himself. One thing must be kept clearly in mind—Jesus wasn't a political revolutionary, although His teaching will revolutionize any man or movement which will earnestly follow it. To Jesus, the enemy wasn't Rome; rather it was the heart of sinful man which produces murder, war, bloodshed, immorality, and corruption. It is sinful man who is mankind's greatest enemy, and the manifestations of the flesh are the same regardless of government.

During the last ten years it has been my privilege to travel through a lot of countries around the world, including countries where Marxist ideologies are the backbone of government, and I have come to the conclusion that there is no such thing as selfless commitment apart from commitment to Jesus Christ. Corruption in government, lust, greed, hate, and deceit are found on both sides of the world, beyond all checkpoints and borders. Christ alone contended to change the heart of man by bringing forgiveness of sin, and with that changed life comes a changed value system—a reason for moral purity and sacrificial courage.

"Since the ideology of atheism," writes Josif Ton, "produces a character that is not essential to a victorious socialism, but on the contrary works against it, why continue to spread it?" Ton believes that Christianity, rather than fading under Marxism, has grown and must be reckoned with. He calls for a revised Communist view of religion, one that recognizes in Christ the fulfillment of its goals and aspirations. While Ton may never live to see it, there will one day come an hour when men beat their swords into plowshares and their spears into pruning hooks, and when that hour comes Christ shall reign forever and ever.

14
Discipleship, 1

"Then he said to them all: 'If anyone would come after me, he must deny himself and take up his cross daily and follow me'" (Luke 9:23). Who was this one to make such a bold statement? He's identified in history as Jesus of Nazareth, but Nazareth was merely the place where He grew up. One day, Jesus put the question to His disciples, saying, "Who do people say the Son of Man is?" (Matt. 16:13). Peter answered, "You are the Christ, the Son of the living God" (Matt. 16:16).

In both Marxist and revolutionary circles Jesus has recently gained new prominence as one who had the courage to be different, as one who greatly changed the course of history. Jesus laid it on the line with His followers. He didn't sugar-coat the challenge. In fact, there were times when He actually made it difficult for men to follow. He believed that a nucleus of really dedicated men and women could accomplish far more than an army of Sunday warriors who tipped their hats to Him on Sunday morning and forgot Him for the rest of the week.

"If anyone would come after me," Jesus challenged, "he must deny himself" (Matt. 16:24). In spite of the revival of religious interest today, the fact that there is very little real denial of self is one of the indications that much of what we call Christianity is superficial and lacking depth of meaning. "Deny yourself and take up your cross!" were the words that immediately brought to people's minds the picture of crucifixion and all that it stood for. The disciples who heard Jesus were aware of what crucifixion was, for on many occasions they had watched as a helpless victim was impaled on wooden timbers affixed at right angles.

The cross spoke of death, hideous, agonizing death, and the disciples immediately recognized that if they would really follow Jesus, then He had to be first as they put their own ambitions and interests aside. Does Jesus demand less today? Does He still insist that His kingdom be put above our own kingdoms of personal gain?

When Wycliffe Bible translator Ken Jacobs tried to translate this word *deny* when he was working with the Chamula Indians of Mexico, he found that in their culture and language, they had no concept of self-denial. Flagellation, or beating themselves—yes, they had a word for that, but to deny self was foreign to them. Finally, Ken translated the word, saying, "If anyone wants to follow me, let him put out of his own heart what his own heart wants to do, and come take up his cross daily and follow me." And that is what discipleship is all about.

One last thought: Following Jesus is totally voluntary. He doesn't coerce men. He doesn't bribe them with "a home in the sky in the sweet by-and-by." He merely invites them to "Come; follow me." He demands one thing, though. He insists on first place.

Contemporary Christianity seems to be afflicted with an AMYF blight: "After me, you're first!" Why not be a Christian? It might even be good for business. But the message of the cross hasn't changed with the passing of time. Carved in ivory or gilded with twenty-four-karat gold, it still speaks of personal

67

death so that Christ may live. Even nature itself teaches us that death must precede life. The seed dies and is buried in the cold earth before new life sprouts within. Today, Jesus asks no less. "If any man would come after me, let him deny himself and take up his cross and follow me" (Mark 8:34, RSV). That is the beginning of life that knows no end.

15
Discipleship, 2

Adoniram Judson, the great missionary to Burma, wrote a tract in Burmese. He predicted, "About one or two hundred years hence the religion of Buddha, Brahma, and all other false religions will disappear and the religion of Christ will pervade the whole world." We have not only passed the first century mark from the time that Judson wrote those words, but we are also rapidly approaching the second century mark, and the sad fact is that there are far more men and women today who have no idea of who Jesus Christ is than there were alive in Judson's time.

As the population has continued to skyrocket, the task of confronting a world with the claims of Jesus Christ has continued to grow. I have no doubt that Judson was sincere, but his prediction didn't come true because everyone didn't have the burning desire to share his faith that Judson had. Today vast numbers of the world's population have little idea of who Jesus really is. No less than 250 million boys and girls in China are under ten years of age—a vast army larger in size than the entire population of the United States—and to them Jesus Christ is only a Western religious figure.

Why is it that so many today are uncertain when it comes to sharing their faith, unwilling to do more than wave the flag? Could it be that we have identified with Jesus Christ as we do with a political party? Could it be that the turmoil in places such as Ireland, where one group is pitted against another group, exists because we have merely called ourselves Christians without understanding what it means to follow Jesus?

I'm thinking of a youngster who walked into the living room one day and announced, "Mother, I'm nine feet tall—just as tall as Goliath who fought David." The mother smiled as she looked down at her small fry, who barely reached her waist. "And how did you figure out that you are nine feet tall?"

asked the mother. "Oh," said the little boy, "I went into the bedroom and took some cardboard and made me a ruler and measured myself. See—nine feet tall!"

What is the measure of a real disciple, a real follower of Jesus Christ? The number of times he goes to church, or the amount of money he gives in a year? Is it his frequency in attending Mass or saying the rosary?

When the Communists took over in China, Sam Moffatt was arrested and thrown in prison. One day, thinking of the turmoil that had come to that country and of his own fate, he asked one of his captors, "What chance is there?" The man replied, "None." "Why?" asked Moffatt. "Because they are willing to die for what they believe, and I don't believe you are." That's the answer!

Our crosses have been gilded in twenty-four-karat gold, and its significance has been reduced to a trinket that we wear around our necks. The cross demands commitment—not consideration! Christ asks for no less today than he did nineteen hundred years ago, and it will take the same price to reach our generation that the disciples were willing to pay—everything!

When Charles Lindberg considered flying

the Atlantic, over waters which no other man had ever successfully crossed, he took his map and drew a line which he called the point of no return. After he crossed that point, Lindberg knew there was no turning back, and so it is with the man who means business in following Jesus Christ.

"Must Jesus bear the cross alone/And all the world go free?" asks the songwriter, Thomas Shepherd. "No, there's a cross for ev'ryone/ and there's a cross for me."

16
Discipleship, 3

He stood apart from the crowd, yet he wasn't aloof, better than others. He was warm, compelling, and controversial. His eyes could flash fire, yet they mellowed with affection. Children loved Him, yet others felt that His look completely stripped them of the veneer of respectability. His name was Jesus, and the way He approached things was so different from the way men build organizations today. Christ taught that a small group of men who were really dedicated to His cause could accomplish far more than could a vast army of Sunday warriors who were committed only to their own little kingdoms.

Jesus often talked about discipleship, and the concept encompasses the whole gamut of commitment. A study of what He said answers the question, "What is a disciple?"

First, Jesus said a disciple is a follower. "Take up your cross and follow me!" Jesus told His disciples. If there is a secret to the Christian life, it is the secret of daily renewal, of daily taking up the cross to follow Him. "The inward man," wrote Paul, "is renewed day by day" (II Cor. 4:16, KJV). Following Christ is merely a matter of living each day, walking in His footsteps.

Second, said Jesus, a disciple is a learner. It is interesting to note that the Greek word for "disciple," *mathētēs*, comes from the word *manthano*, which means "to learn." Hence, a true disciple is a learner—one who is instructed by the Holy Spirit.

How much do you really know of God's Word? Would you put yourself in the company of those who thought the epistles were the wives of the apostles? Can you name the Old Testament poetical books? Have you any idea who wrote the Book of Hebrews, or why? If the Bible is our textbook, our manual for spiritual survival, we had better have more than a passing acquaintance with it.

In my garden is a lovely bonsai olive tree—all of eighteen inches tall. It is perfectly formed but dwarfed, and it will never be much taller than it is today. Years ago the Japanese discovered that if the root of a plant is cut and the branches are trained properly, you can produce a miniature—a plant that is fully formed but never gains full maturity or growth. That's the picture of a vast army of contemporary Christians—bonsais who have never attained the full measure of Christ.

Third, said Jesus, a disciple is a lover. He must love his Master so much that his love for everything and everyone else is as but hatred. "Anyone who loves his father or mother more than me," said Jesus, "is not worthy of me; anyone who loves his son or daughter more than me is not worthy of me" (Matt. 10:37).

Finally, Jesus announced that a disciple is one who has made Christ his true measure of life and values. David Livingstone, the son of a Scottish miller, had as his life motto the words, "I will place no value on anything I have or possess except in its relationship to the kingdom of God."

Disciples are both born and made! We are born a disciple when we are born again and begin to follow Jesus, but we are made as we live one day at a time, confessing our sin and failure, and striving to walk in the footsteps of

Jesus. A disciple isn't a perfect man or woman; he has merely begun to follow a Savior who is perfect in love and humility. We're walking in His footsteps and by God's grace, and although we may stumble, we're going to get up and keep on following Jesus. That's what discipleship is all about!

Part Three

Great Lives Demonstrate Christianity Works

17
Augustine

Amidst the crumbling ruins of the Roman Empire in 354, one of the greatest champions of Christian faith was born in a small North African province. His name was Augustine. In capsule form, here is his biography.

As a youth, Augustine was reared in the church of his day, although at first the church seemed to make no great impression on him. His mother was a Christian; his father was a noble Roman. In his late teen years Augustine —like many of our twentieth-century collegians—turned to philosophy, and under its influence he turned from the church. His heart was seeking for an answer to the questions of life. At first he thought he found peace in a pagan religion called Manicheanism, but soon Augustine was seized with doubt and agnosticism. For a time he drifted and doubted, still seeking anchors for his restless heart.

In his autobiography, *Confessions*, Augustine tells about this period of great turmoil and unrest. He indicates that he shared in the vices and corruptions of his day. For a number of years he lived a life of immorality. Then quite suddenly in 387 Augustine found faith in God through Jesus Christ His Son. Augustine's seeking heart found an answer that has satisfied the restlessness of men in all ages.

Many people today lead lives that parallel the life of Augustine—born in the shadow of a church, reared in a Christian atmosphere, in college years confronted with periods of doubt and unbelief. But the restless seekings of the human heart in this twentieth century can still find peace through faith in Jesus Christ.

Why is Augustine important? In spite of the life that he lived before he found Christian faith, he made one of the greatest contributions to Christianity that has been made since the time of the apostle Paul. He is one of the few men in history who is equally loved and respected by Catholics and Protestants.

Augustine experienced the depths of sin, yet he found that the grace of God is greater than the greatest sin. Augustine's approach to Christian faith began with his assertion that the human heart is entirely corrupted by sin, which he defined as "choosing our own way rather than God's way." He believed that man was created perfect, but that in the Garden of Eden man rejected God and fell to the depths of degradation. He believed all men have sinned and come short of God's standard. He said there is nothing in the heart of man that is worthy of God and that all we could ever do would never bring us to a place where we could be worthy of the Savior.

Augustine held that only by the grace of God could anyone find eternal life. And he was right, for the apostle Paul said, "For by grace are ye saved through faith; and that not of yourselves: it is the gift of God: not of works, lest any man should boast" (Eph. 2:8-9, KJV). Augustine's life was really no different from the life of countless thousands today—seeking, restless, drifting. In his *Confessions*, Augustine wrote, "Thou hast made us for Thyself, O God, and our heart is restless until it finds its rest in Thee." In relation to

Augustine's life, where are you? Have you found reality in Jesus Christ—or are you still seeking? You, like Augustine, can discover that the answer is not in sin, loose living, or philosophy, but in a personal relationship to Jesus Christ.

18

Brother Lawrence

There are few people in the world who can honestly say that God disappointed them, yet Nicholas Herman was one of them. He was converted to Christianity at the age of eighteen. Seeing a dry, leafless tree in the dead of winter and realizing that soon it would burst forth into life as the sap rose in the spring, Herman knew that he was spiritually dead and asked God to give him a rebirth. It happened, too, and for a time Nicholas Herman served as a footman and a soldier.

In 1666, Nicholas Herman entered a monastic order, expecting to suffer a great deal at the hand of God as the result of his prior sinful life, but God disappointed him. Instead of a life of regret and suffering, Herman, who was given the name of Brother Lawrence, found forgiveness, joy, and peace beyond expectation. Brother Lawrence's faith, however, was soon put to the test, for he was assigned to the kitchen. By nature Lawrence was awkward and clumsy. Kitchen duty was a challenge, but the way that he tackled it provides guidelines for living even in this century.

Lawrence believed that even the most mundane and worldly task can be done in love for God, and doing it for the great King gives the most humble task spiritual purpose. In *Practicing the Presence of Christ*, Brother Lawrence shares what God taught him. He wrote, "The time of business does not with me differ from the time of prayer, and in the noise and clatter of my kitchen while several persons are at the same time caling for different things, I possess God in as great tranquillity as if I were upon my knees. . . ."

How did Lawrence approach his duty as cook for the brotherhood? With prayer! He wrote that he began each task with fervent prayer and then tackled it with love for God. At the end of the meal, he prayed again with thanksgiving. Lawrence wrote, "We ought not to be weary of doing little things for the love of God, who regards not the greatness of the work, but the love with which it is performed."

To Brother Lawrence, the practical aspects of Christianity could be summed up in three words from the pen of the apostle Paul: faith, hope, love. Lawrence said, "All things are possible to him who believes, that they are less difficult to him who hopes; that they are more easy to him who loves, and still more easy to him who perseveres in the practice of these three virtues." What a legacy! Putting faith, hope, and love into operation was to Brother Lawrence practicing the presence of God.

Most family arguments occur not in the bedroom, but in the kitchen, thirty minutes before the evening meal, when the members of the family converge, warm, tired, and tense. You, like Brother Lawrence, may hate kitchen duty. It may be a wearisome drudgery to you. Then learn his secret and do it with love for the Lord. Lawrence's practical approach to the presence of Christ is biblical. "And whatsoever ye do," wrote Paul to the Colossians, "do it heartily, as to the Lord, and not unto men" (Col. 3:23, KJV).

What is the thing that you most dread doing? Whatever your answer, this is your challenge, and applying a generous dose of the presence of Christ in the form of faith, hope, and love can transform it into a work of grace. There is no difference between the secular and the sacred, for all things can become sacred. As Brother Lawrence, who lived to be more than eighty, wrote, "Practicing the presence of God is the best rule of a holy life."

19
Olga Robertson

How many men can one woman love? More than one woman has wrestled with that question, and this chapter will not give you a definitive answer, but I have come to conclude that one woman can love at least nine thousand men. This woman's name is Olga Robertson and she's affectionately known as Mommie Olga to the nine thousand men who are inmates of new Bilibid Prison outside of the city of Manila in the Philippines.

Unquestionably, Olga qualifies as one of the most interesting women you'd ever meet anywhere. She's an unusual contradiction of what you'd expect to find in a woman, which is part of the reason she has a heart big enough to love so many men—many of whom are rather unlovable. Olga bears an

American passport, but actually she's Lebanese. She's reached the age where most women settle down and begin to think of leisure and grandchildren, but Mommie Olga is a dynamic bundle of energy with projects going all directions at once, from the supervision of a new chapel for prison guards to seeing that none with a spiritual need is turned away.

Most women would be frightened to move freely among tough convicts in one of the world's largest prisons, where gangs are part of survival. She says she's really a "scaredy-cat." But the fact that she has spent almost eighteen years as spiritual counselor and advisor at Bilibid belies the claim that she's afraid of anything. Olga's thin frame, her dancing dark eyes, and bouncing steps have endeared her to the hearts of men who see very little of women. But Olga is a special kind of woman. She has a powerful weapon working for her, the kind that criminologists and law-enforcement officials would do well to study—it is the power of an old-fashioned, dynamic love that changes lives for good . . . and for God.

I was with Olga recently and saw first-hand

how God's love through Olga had transformed the lives of men who had been murderers, rapists, homosexuals, and hardened criminals. But that is all gone and their lives have been drastically changed. As the men lined up to get their sample of after-shave lotion, doled out personally by Mommie Olga, I saw not criminals but men who laughed and joked and reflected a tenderness that is rare anywhere—especially in a prison. Their eyes glistened with tears as they sang and testified that Jesus Christ had changed their lives.

As I sat there and pondered the forceful impact of one lone woman plus God, I couldn't help thinking that the human heart is an amazing thing. When a person is in love with himself, there is little room to love anybody else. Greed, selfishness, misery, and unhappiness are the symptoms of a self-centered love, but when you are really in love with Christ, you can love an infinite number of other people— yes, even nine thousand men. I saw that gleam, that indefinable dynamic love of Christ in her eyes as Olga said, "God loves them, and so do I." Hers isn't a sentimental love, but the kind that is durable and tough enough to take her to the side of the electric chair as men paid society's price for their crimes. That's the transforming power of God's love in a heart big enough to love others as Christ has loved us in a loveless world.

20
Malcolm Muggeridge

When World War II broke out, Malcolm Muggeridge was chief of British Intelligence in Mozambique. Toward the end of the war, Muggeridge became depressed and decided to end his life. He swam out to sea, never intending to return, but this mission turned out to be one of the few failures of his life. Something happened that Muggeridge can't explain in natural terms. He saw a brilliant light which he described as "an ecstatic illumination." Almost without realizing what he was doing, he turned around and headed for shore. He made it . . . barely.

Today Muggeridge looks back and feels that he turned the corner that day and began traveling toward Christianity, but when he got there isn't really clear to this British-born journalist whose sense of clarity has both shocked and thrilled the English-speaking world.

Covering the 1954 Billy Graham crusade may have been another milestone toward faith, and certainly Muggeridge's time spent with Mother Teresa in India contributed to his conversion. Like his former countryman, the scholar C. S. Lewis, there wasn't a single event or moment that resulted in Muggeridge's conversion to Christ. He describes it as "a process, not a sudden Damascus-Road experience, but more like the journeying of Bunyan's Pilgrim who constantly lost his way, fell into the sloughs, was locked up in the Doubting Castle and terrified out of his wits in the Valley of the Shadow of Death. But still, through it all," he says, "[I] had a sense of moving toward the light. . . ."

Now in his late seventies, Muggeridge has found the Light and is following in the footsteps of Lewis, C. E. M. Joad, and scores of others—men who were skeptical and agnostic but gradually came to realize Christianity offers the only real hope of the world. "It would be very difficult," says Muggeridge, "for anybody looking around the world today to resist the conclusion that something has gone very badly awry with what we continue to call Western civilization."

In his newest book, *Christ and the Media*, Muggeridge tells how he is constantly beseiged for an explanation as to why someone with his experience and his intellectual credentials would opt for Jesus Christ rather than Marx or D. H. Lawrence. His answer isn't emotional; nor is it only intellectual. In the incarnation (when Jesus Christ became man), Muggeridge sees the only real hope for humanity. "The incarnation," he says, "gives man courage and insight to be an individual . . . God reaches down to become a man; a man reaches up to become God in order that man may comprehend the nature of his relationship with his Creator."

Malcolm Muggeridge will die as a man who has made peace with His Creator and with himself. In *Christ and the Media*, he said, "As the old do, I often wake up in the night, half out of my body, so that I see between the sheets the old battered carcass I shall soon be leaving for good, and in the distance a glow in the sky, the lights of Augustine's City of God." In this he sees himself as "a participant in His purposes, which are loving, not malign, orderly not chaotic,—and in that certainty a great peace and a great joy."

Thus Malcolm Muggeridge summarizes his faith and trust—the kind that God intends for all men to have. May God give us many more Malcolm Muggeridges—men of ability who have come to grips with the reality of the resurrected Christ.

21
George Müller

George Müller was educated in the universities of Germany during the time when
rationalism was the dominant philosophy.
Rationalism is a humanistic philosophy that
leaves God pretty much on the sidelines of
life, and certainly Müller did that very thing
for the first twenty years of his life. As a
young man, Müller's pleasures consisted of
wine, women, and song. He ended up in jail,
to the shame of his father and family who
wanted their son to become a clergyman.
Müller wanted anything but that!

At the age of twenty, while studying at the
university, Müller was invited to the home of
a friend who was a Christian. That evening,
Müller was intrigued to see his friend kneel
and pray, something which Müller had never

seen before. Following the meal, the host read a chapter from the Bible—the same chapter that Müller's professor ridiculed. The reading of Scripture was followed by a hymn. Müller felt so awkward that he apologized for even being there, but that night changed his life. When he wrote his autobiography, Müller couldn't remember if it was that night that he went home and knelt down for the first time to pray as he had seen his friend Graham Wagner do; but it is certain that Müller was shortly thereafter converted to Jesus Christ, and when he was, Müller quickly learned the secret of prayer.

In the university, Müller had excelled as a scholar, and with the same fervent dedication he now turned to the Scriptures and began to apply them to his life. Rejecting a rationalistic approach to life, Müller believed that faith is believing the promises of God and then standing upon them completely. At the same time, Müller began to be concerned for the orphans who wandered the streets of Bristol, England, where he was pastor of a church. This was the beginning of the orphanages that Müller established—which were operated on the principle of faith in God.

During his lifetime, George Müller never asked for money for his work, yet in response to his faith, God sent the equivalent of much more than $1 million. There were times when there was no food, yet Müller would not allow his staff to send out a plea for money—unlike some organizations today. Instead, Müller would go into his room and bend his knees in prayer. Often Müller would instruct, "Set the table for dinner," although there was nothing to cook. He would then go to pray . . . and God provided. In a world of ICBMs and bombs measured in megatons, a world when much happens in the Christian world as the result of good promotions and clever psychology, we need to rediscover the power of the bended knee—the power of prayer.

When Müller was in his eighties, he was asked to speak to a group of seminary students. One of them raised his hand as the old man finished his address and said, "Mr. Müller, there is a question which some of us would like to ask." "Yes," said Müller as he strained to listen. "What is your secret?" the student asked. The eighty-year-old man asked that the question be repeated. "What is your secret?" Müller pushed his chair back and began to bend his old, cold limbs to the floor, kneeling in prayer. "This is the secret," replied Müller. One of his biographers wrote that when he died, it was discovered that there were two ridges or grooves cut into the wooden floor at his bedside. Müller had literally worn two depressions into the wooden floor as he knelt beside his bed in prayer.

Have you discovered the power of the bended knee? The same God who heard the prayers of a man who rejected human explanations to life is alive today and will answer your prayer. "And this is the confidence that we have in him," wrote the apostle John, "that, if we ask any thing according to his will, He heareth us" (I John 5:14, KJV). May God help us to discover the power of the bended knee.

22
Hannah Whitall Smith

In *The Christian's Secret of a Happy Life*, Hannah Whitall Smith relates a story about the time a skeptic came to her and said, "You Christians seem to have a religion that makes you miserable. You are like a man with a headache. He does not want to get rid of his head, but it hurts him to keep it. You cannot expect outsiders to seek very earnestly for anything so uncomfortable." Then, wrote Hannah Smith, she discovered that Christianity ought to make a person happy, not miserable, and began to ask the Lord to show her what that secret is.

Many people today are like the man with a headache—they don't want to get rid of their faith, but they feel that it makes them miserable and that being a Christian keeps them from having a really good time. I am thinking of the young woman who wrote to her mother and said that she was miserable because, by not sleeping with the boys who dated her in college, they dropped her quickly. "Goodness" was making her miserable.

How about it? Is God a cosmic killjoy who has given us a black book full of rules and regulations to keep us out of hell but takes the happiness out of life in the meanwhile?

Hannah Whitall Smith faced this very problem and what she discovered she put into a book which has become a classic, with more than two million copies in circulation. She contends that many people have been saved from the penalty of their sin, but not from its power. They are still attracted by the glamor and the bright lights—like the girl who felt that keeping her virginity came with the price tag of loneliness.

The secret, discovered Hannah Smith, is accepting the fact that God will never ask you to give up something without giving something of far greater value and worth. But, like the acrobat who swings from trapeze to trapeze overhead, you must turn loose of the one before you can grasp the next. In other words—for the believer to be hid with Christ in God, as Smith puts it—you must be willing to make a commitment of yourself to Christ which is more than salvation. Consecration, as she calls it, is putting yourself in the hands of Him who made you and who knows what is best for your life.

Smith once explained this concept to a doctor by saying, "Doctor, suppose that you had a patient who wanted you to make him well, but he refused to take the medicine that you prescribed, and he also refused to tell you just where he hurt and what had happened. Could you do your best for him?" "Of course not," replied the doctor. Neither can God do a complete work in our lives if we are willing to give Him only token allegiance or commitment.

The secret of a happy Christian life is that the power of God can work within so that our lives become the outworking of His Spirit. The man or woman who tries to find happiness by shutting God out of his life will always have a hollowness within, a void or an emptiness which can never be filled or deadened by the taste of fame and fortune. In simple terms—God made you for Himself, and you will never be happier than you will be in the center of His will, letting Him work through you to accomplish His purpose.

Are you like the man with a headache? You know what is right, but you are afraid that doing it will cost you. Some of the most miserable people I've ever met are those who have been inoculated by the Gospel. They have just enough to make them miserable, but not enough to do them any good. Real happiness comes only by being in His will, in His time, and His place.

Part Four

The Principles
of Success

23
People Who Didn't Succeed

Scattered around the world on beaches and at resorts are the crumpled yellow boxes which once contained Kodak film, and strangely enough the life of the man who made "Kodak" a household word ended his life almost like the crumpled box that was carelessly tossed on the beach. His name was George Eastman of the Eastman-Kodak Company. Eastman popularized the idea, "You click the shutter, we do the rest." And that idea turned rags to riches as the Scandinavian-born inventor became a multimillionaire.

Eastman lived in a great thirty-room mansion, where he had a pipe organ installed and hired an organist to play during meals. None could deny that Eastman was successful, but he wasn't happy. He became a depressed, discouraged man. One day he had breakfast as the organist played, conferred with his associates, and then went to his bedroom where he shut the door, sat down at his desk, and wrote, "My work is finished. Why wait?" Then he took a Luger automatic pistol, and shot himself.

Financial success came to Eastman, but it takes far more than that to bring real happiness to a person. What is success? Fame, fortune, prestige, influence? Or something entirely different? Is it possible that we have missed the real meaning and purpose of success, and that some who have learned what success really is are far from being considered successful in terms of wealth or popularity?

Take, for instance, Oswald Chambers. As a young Scot, Chambers showed real promise of becoming one of Europe's top artists. He obtained his Art Masters' certificate at the age of eighteen and was invited to study in Europe under some of his day's great masters, but Chambers turned the offer down. Having seen others who became spiritually shipwrecked in the universities of Europe, he chose rather to go to the University of Edinburgh, where he majored in art and archaeology. Shortly thereafter, this young man began to consider success in the light of God's direction. He then enrolled in a small Bible school in Dunoon, Scotland. Later Chambers went to Egypt, where he died at the age of twenty-five.

Some people cried, "What a wasted life! What great talent gone to waste!" Yet Chambers saw success in terms of finding and doing the will of God for his life. He wrote, "I am not many kinds of fools in one. I am only one kind of fool—the kind that believes and obeys God." There are thousands of men and women like Chambers who have found that real success—the kind that brings joy and happiness in life—is found by giving, not by getting.

In the upper room, Jesus took a towel and a basin and performed the service of a slave as He washed the feet of His disciples. Then said Jesus, "Happy are ye if ye do [these things]" (John 13:17, KJV). Real success—success as God sees it—cannot be measured in terms of monetary gain, or influence and prestige. It can only be measured in terms of God's will for our lives and how we do His bidding.

To halt the number of suicides on a particularly tall bridge, authorities recommended the construction of a "jumpproof" fence. When they did, Dr. Jesse Carr of the University of California Medical Center said men commit suicide because they don't like the life they are living and you can't talk them out of it. Said this prominent psychiatrist, "You have to change that kind of life and give them a new one."

If that's the way you feel, there's good news. Christ can change your life and make it worth living. Life without God becomes vain, empty, and shallow. It is without purpose and meaning, without definition or goals, but life with a spiritual dimension spells success which endures.

24
When Your Goal
Is Success

Is success a truly worthy goal? That, of course, depends on your definition of success. Nearly thirty-four hundred years ago, an assembly of rugged men stood before the Jordan River as they were about to cross into the Promised Land. For forty years these weathered nomads had wandered in the wilderness. But at last their hour had come. The only mention of the word *success* in the King James Version is found in the charge that God gave to those pilgrims. It's found in Joshua 1:8. To these people God promised success if they would walk in the light of His revealed Word, turning neither to the right nor to the left.

Are those principles just as valid today when two spaceships rendezvous somewhere between the earth and the moon, and most of the people on earth can be linked by satellite communications? Does God really have something to say about success? In the pages of His Word, the Bible, men have found not only how to make a living, but how to live as well.

God's formula is unchanging in a changing world because it deals with principles that are not subject to winds of fluctuation. God views success in terms of being, not having, giving, or grabbing. Do you want to be a real success? Then begin by taking God as your partner in life.

Does God have anything to do with prosperity? Well, John W. Yates, along with John D. Rockefeller, R. G. LeTourneau, and a host of others, believes He does. Yates was a fifteen-year-old boy, the son of a tenant farmer, when he walked into a bank and asked to open an account. When the banker asked how he wanted the account made out, Yates replied, "John W. Yates and Company, sir."

The banker, who had known John since he was a little boy, smiled as he said, "And who is the company, John?" Without batting an eyelash, John replied, "God is." The checks of that boy who stood there with three layers of cardboard in the soles of his shoes later were honored for $10 million. He believed a man could enter into partnership with God through a personal experience with Jesus Christ.

The second guideline for being a real success is to begin to follow God's directions for successful living as found in the pages of Scripture. Jesus said plainly, "But seek first his kingdom and his righteousness, and all these things will be given to you as well" (Matt. 6:33). He further taught that success can't be equated with financial gain because, said Jesus, "A man's life does not consist in the abundance of his possessions" (Luke 12:15).

The Bible is an ageless textbook on living that teaches men what some of the world's wealthiest individuals have never learned— the great lesson of learning how to live. If you are serious about being a success as God views success, then turn your life and resources over to God, allowing Him to direct the affairs of your business.

Oh, you're afraid the business might go bankrupt? That didn't happen to John D. Rockefeller, Sr., who became one of the world's wealthiest men. Rockefeller acknowledged God's direction by returning a tithe or a tenth of all his income to the Lord. When asked if he tithed his income, Rockefeller replied, "Yes, I tithe. And I want to say, if I had not tithed the first dollar I made, I would not have tithed the first million."

You see, you really can't outgive God when He's your partner in life.

25
Attempt Great
Things for God

Interested in being successful in your profession? If you answer yes, you're normal, and your answer doesn't reflect selfishness or greed. The desire to be a success is normal enough—this is a desire that has been put there by God Himself. In recent years, many books have been written about success—for example, Napoleon Hill's *Think and Grow Rich* and Frank Betgger's *How I Raised Myself from Failure to Success in Selling.*

Another book which deals with success is the Bible, and it deals with success in terms of being rather than just having. This great textbook on living says that to be a real success, it is necessary to have a personal relationship with God through Jesus Christ whereby we enter into a partnership with God and begin to follow the directions found in the pages of Scripture.

In this book, God promises to bless the endeavor of a man who will follow His direction. Success, as the Bible defines it, is seeking and finding the will of God for your life. Having begun to follow the Bible's principles, determine what it is that God wants you to accomplish. Discover where God wants you to ultimately go and don't ask, "How will I get there?" God promises, "Trust in the Lord with all your heart and lean not on your own understanding; in all your ways acknowledge him, and he will make your paths straight" (Prov. 3:5-6).

Napoleon Hill does make a significant statement that is true of the man who has found out where God wants him to go. He says, "What the mind of man can conceive and believe, it can achieve." Do you believe that? Paul did, for he wrote, "I can do everything through him who gives me strength" (Phil. 4:13). Have you ever given any serious thought to what God's plan is for your life? Don't dwell on the negative factors such as your social background or your lack of money to get through medical school. Rather discover what is God's goal for your life as the first step. A multitude of voices will say, "It can't be done," but with God's help it can be done.

Many of the accomplishments of our day have been made over the objections of those who said it couldn't be done. One of the men I most admire in the field of medicine is a German doctor by the name of Werner Forssman. At the age of twenty-five, Forssman terrified his professors in medical school by suggesting that a rubber tube be worked through a vein into the heart, which would then be x-rayed. They were convinced it would kill a man and forbade that he conduct the experiment.

Forssman was convinced otherwise. He cut a vein in his left arm and worked a rubber tube down into his heart. Then he walked into the x-ray room and took an x-ray of his own heart. That process was the forerunner of the modern process of heart catheterization, which has saved thousands of lives.

Do you believe that God wants you to become a successful businessman? Then roll your sleeves up and get to work. Do you believe God wants you to build the largest church in your city? Then start knocking on doors and meeting the needs of people. Are you convinced that God wants you to do what others think impossible? Then remember the words of William Carey, whose life motto was, "Attempt great things for God, expect great things from God."

There is a closing thought as I share this important guideline with you—the man who has a goal is like a fish that swims upstream. Very few people know where they are going in life. When you know where you want to go, you'll baffle some folks and others won't like it. But if you will quietly begin to work toward God under God, you will find that He will begin to open doors as you trust Him. Others may rush by you pell-mell, but in the long run, speed isn't the important thing—it is direction that really counts.

26
The Rusty Keys
of Success

The keys to success are not scarce—they are simply rusty through misuse and neglect. One of those keys is to discover what God really wants you to accomplish in life, realizing that nothing is impossible to him who believes and works. The second key to success, as revealed in the pages of Scripture, is to discipline your life in reaching toward that goal.

The apostle Paul, many people believe, was not only a great success in his endeavors, but also had in his life the determination to be successful no matter what he did. Significant are his words to the Philippians (3:13, KJV). "This one thing I do"—not a half-dozen things or even two. "This one thing I do" spoke of his resolute determination to accomplish his goal. Equally importantly, Paul disciplined his life.

When G. Keith Funston was president of the New York Stock Exchange, he said the most important advice ever given to him came from his mother, who once told him, "When you know you should do something, *do it!*" Success often lies just beyond the grasp of people who cannot discipline their lives to stay with something. Not only do they find it hard to get started, but they also get discouraged easily and hop from one thing to another.

To the Corinthians, Paul stressed the need of discipline when he compared the Christian life to the race of the Greek athlete. "I beat my body and make it my slave," he wrote to them, "so that after I have preached to others, I myself will not be disqualified for the prize" (I Cor. 9:27). If you know you should do something, do it now, and stay with it no matter how long it takes.

Another important guideline in striving towards success is the ability to profit from your failures. I am firmly persuaded that in your failure, if you will listen, you can hear the voice of God saying, "Listen, you've strayed from the right path, and I let this hap-

118

pen to you so that you will move back into the center of my will."

The Old Testament king of Israel, Saul, was a typical example. With great physical stature and personality, he had everything going for him. When he was crowned king, he began well but soon started to fail. First he disregarded God's direction and started making his own rules, which resulted in God's rebuke. But this failure was compounded by further disobedience, with the result that his sons were barred from ever becoming king. Shortly before his death, these words fell from the man who had great opportunity—"I have acted like a fool and have erred greatly" (I Sam. 26:21).

The successful man learns from his failures. As someone said, "He climbs the ladder of success wrong by wrong." Failure and setbacks offer the opportunity to discover God's redirection. Actually, opportunity may come slipping in by the back door, disguised in the form of misfortune or temporary defeat, which accounts for the fact that so many people never recognize opportunity.

Thomas Edison, the man who invented the incandescent light, is an outstanding example of someone who didn't quit in the face of failure. When he had tried more than ten thousand experiments, trying to produce an incandescent light, friends said, "Edison, why don't you quit? It just can't be done." He retorted, "I've found out ten thousand ways it cannot be done. Now I will find out how it can be done." And he did!

When failure knocks, ask God to give new direction and purpose. Then keep on doing the will of God from your heart with determination to let nothing stop you.

27
The True Mark
of a Man

What is the true mark of a man? His age, his worth, his ideas, or his accomplishment?

To the Eastern mind, man is often measured by the length of his beard or the white of his hair. Thus wisdom, in the Orient, is synonymous with age. Yet history tells us that age is not necessarily the true mark of a man.

To the businessman worth is often considered to be the true mark of a man. We say this person is worth a cool million—meaning that he is worth a million dollars. How he made that money isn't important. It may have been through dishonest and deceitful business practices. When we stop and think about life we have to conclude that worth is not necessarily the true mark of a man.

The philosopher would suggest that a man's ideas are his true mark. And who can overestimate the power of an idea? Victor Hugo, the French author, recognized the great power of thought when he said, "Greater than the tread of mighty armies is an idea whose time has come." Notice how the ideas of Karl Marx and Lenin changed the course of history. Would you say that a man's ideas are his true mark?

The pragmatist would say, "Away with ideas. Away with the dreamer and the visionary." He would say, "Show me what a man has done and I will show you his true mark." The pragmatist is interested in accomplishment. Would you say accomplishment is the true mark of a man?

How do you suppose God looks at man? What measure does God use in determining the true mark of a man—his true greatness? I think we would all agree that in these days of greed, pressure, and exploitation, surely God views life from a different perspective. What does God use for the measure of a man?

Try these words as guidelines for living. "Blessed is the man who does not walk in the counsel of the wicked, or stand in the way of sinners or sit in the seat of mockers. But his delight is in the law of the Lord, and on his law he meditates day and night" (Ps. 1:1-2).

God's perspective is certainly a different perspective from ours. We are often caught in the trap of materialism and pragmatism. We put the emphasis on *doing*; God puts it on *being*. We put the emphasis on *accomplishment*; God puts it on *character*. Here's something to consider: What you are is far more important than what you will ever do—whether you are president of the world's largest bank or whether you sweep the street in the smallest city in the world. In the sight of God, being is more important than doing.

Stop and view life in a different perspective—the perspective of eternity—and realize that what you are is more important than what you do. What are you, anyway? A person worth thousands of dollars or even millions, yet a failure from His perspective? Or a person of humble means as the world evaluates your bank account, yet a real success in the eyes of God? What would you say is the real measure of a man? His accomplishments or his character? God is looking for men of character and intergrity who will stand and be counted.

Years ago God spoke through Ezekiel, saying, "I looked for a man among them who

123

would build up the wall and stand before me in the gap . . ." (Ezek. 22:30). God is still looking for men and women of a special kind, and with His help you can be that person.

May I repeat what I wrote several years ago in the preface to *Guidelines for Successful Living:*

> Success means many things to many people; but to me success is equated with neither fame, wealth, nor power. It cannot be measured in the size of bank accounts or the number of trophies of achievement. Real success is finding the will of God and performing His bidding to the greatest potential. Robert Louis Stevenson's searching observation is very appropriate for today: "No one is a success until he writes at the top of the page of his life, 'Enter God.'"